Discover
South Africa

Chris Ward

PowerKiDS
press

Mishawaka-Penn-Harris
Public Library
Mishawaka, Indiana

Published in 2010 by The Rosen Publishing Group Inc.
29 East 21st Street, New York, NY 10010

First Edition

Concept design: Jason Billin
Editor: Susan Crean
Designer: Paul Manning
Consultant: Rob Bowden

Library of Congress Cataloging-in-Publication Data

Ward, Chris, 1973-
  Discover South Africa / Chris Ward.
      p. cm. -- (Discover countries)
  Includes index.
  ISBN 978-1-61532-289-3 (library binding)
  ISBN 978-1-61532-299-2 (paperback)
  ISBN 978-1-61532-300-5 (6-pack)
  1. South Africa--Juvenile literature. I. Title.
  DT1719.W53 2010
  968--dc22

                          2009023735

Photographs:
t=top b=bottom l=left r=right
1, EASI-Images/Roy Maconachie; 3t, Shutterstock/ShutterVision; 3b, Shutterstock/David Peta; 4 (map), Stefan Chabluk; 5,
iStockphoto/Ken Sorrie; 6, BigStockPhoto/Tuckerb34; 7, Photoshot/NIGEL J DENNIS/NHPA; 8, EASI-Images/Roy Maconachie; 9,
Corbis/Gideon Mendel; 10, Shutterstock/Korobanovä; 11, EASI-Images/Roy Maconachie; 12, Corbis/David Turnley; 13,
Corbis/Gideon Mendel; 14, Corbis/Dallas Morning News/Tom Fox; 15, EASI-Images/Roy Maconachie; 16, Corbis/Gideon Mendel;
17, EASI-Images/Roy Maconachie; 18, EASI-Images/Roy Maconachie; 19, Corbis/Nik Wheeler; 20, Corbis/Michael S. Lewis; 21,
Istockphoto/Don Bayley; 22, Shutterstock/PhotoSky 4t com; 23, Corbis/Annie Griffiths/ Belt; 24, Corbis/Martin Harvey; 25, World
Pictures/Photoshot/Roy de la Harpe; 26, Shutterstock/David Peta; 27; Shutterstock/ShutterVision; 28, iStockphoto/Jane Lee
Winter; 29t, EASI-Images/Roy Maconachie; 29b, EASI-Images/Tony Binns
Front cover images: Shutterstock/MaxPhoto; Shutterstock/David Peta.

Manufactured in China
CPSIA Compliance Information: Batch #WAW0102PK: For Further Information
contact Rosen Publishing, New York, New York at 1-800-237-9932

Contents

Discovering South Africa

South Africa, located at the southern tip of the African continent, is slightly less than twice the size of Texas. It is a country of great natural resources which help to make it Africa's strongest economy.

New beginnings

In 1950, the South African government introduced a system called apartheid. It segregated people of different skin color. It gave white people the best land, jobs, schools, and hospitals. Nonwhite people were made to live in other areas and given many fewer facilities.

South Africa Statistics

Area: 470,010 sq. miles (1,219,912 sq. km)

Capital city: Pretoria

Government type: Republic

Bordering countries: Botswana, Lesotho, Mozambique, Namibia, Swaziland, Zimbabwe

Currency: Rand (R)

Language: IsiZulu 23.8%, IsiXhosa 17.6%, Afrikaans 13.3%, Sepedi 9.4%, English 8.2%, Setswana 8.2%, Sesotho 7.9%, Xitsonga 4.4%, other 7.2%

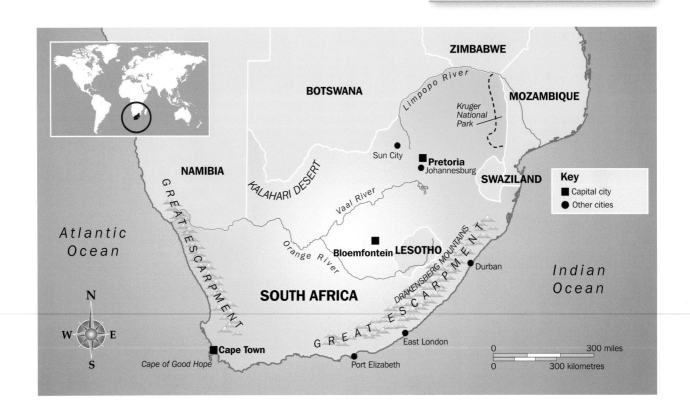

Apartheid ended in 1994. A government led by Nelson Mandela set in motion a new South Africa. The government made plans to create a society that would give all South Africans equal access to schools, doctors, and jobs. It would also allow all South Africans to choose where they wanted to live.

South Africa's capitals

South Africa is a republic. This is a type of government where people elect others to make decisions for them. It has three branches of government. Each branch rules from a different city, so South Africa has three capitals. The main parliament runs the country on a day-to-day basis. It is based in the administrative capital, Pretoria. Cape Town is the legislative capital. There, another part of government discusses and creates new laws. The laws are kept by a judicial part of government, which is based in Bloemfontein.

○ Cape Town is one of South Africa's largest cities.

Challenges ahead

Since the end of apartheid, South Africa has made great progress as a modern country. Its economy has improved and its people have better access to schools, healthcare, and jobs. But there are still problems caused by the old system of apartheid. There are not enough jobs for everyone, or enough housing.

Landscape and climate

Coastline surrounds much of South Africa. The Atlantic Ocean forms South Africa's southwest border. The Indian Ocean forms its southeast border. Most of South Africa's people live in the coastal areas.

Mountains

Just inland from the coast, a ridge of mountains winds through South Africa. It is called the Great Escarpment. Its highest section is the Drakensberg Mountains. South Africa's highest mountain, Njesuthi, is found here. It is 11,181 feet (3,408 m) high. The Drakensberg Mountains form the border of the landlocked country of Lesotho. This small country is entirely surrounded by South Africa.

Highveld and Lowveld

A vast, highland plateau makes up almost two-thirds of South Africa. Known as the Highveld, it is the least-populated region of the country. The Lowveld surrounds the Highveld and runs along the coast. This low-lying area of land is dry and desertlike in the west. The driest area of the country is in the northwest where part of the Kalahari Desert lies. In the south and east, the Lowveld is more fertile and has higher rainfall. This area of the Lowveld is good for farming.

Facts at a glance

Highest point: Njesuthi 11,181 feet (3,408 m)

Longest river: Orange River 1,300 miles (2,100 km)

Coastline: 1,739 miles (2,798 km)

▼ These people are hiking in the Drakensberg Mountains, the highest peaks in South Africa.

Water

South Africa's main river is the Orange River. It begins in the mountains of Lesotho and flows 1,300 miles (2,100 km) across the Highveld to the Atlantic Ocean in the west. In general, South Africa lacks fresh water and droughts are a regular problem. Most of its other rivers carry any rain that does fall from the Great Escarpment to the Indian Ocean.

⚠ A dust storm strikes the Kalahari Desert. Very few people live there.

Climate

South Africa's climate is linked closely to its landscapes. The Great Escarpment blocks cooling winds and rains that come in off the ocean. This means that the Highveld is generally hot and dry. The highest part of the Highveld, however, is much cooler. Frosts are common during the winter, and there is even enough snow for skiing! Most of the Lowveld region in the east has a warm and wet climate.

DID YOU KNOW?
Table Mountain, the flat-topped mountain overlooking Cape Town, is sometimes covered in a "tablecloth." That is the name for the cloud and mist that hides the top of the mountain.

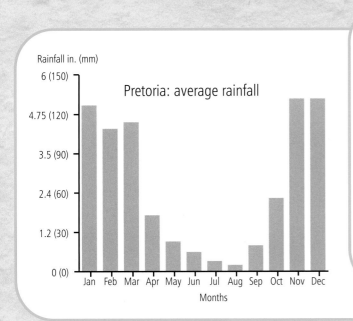

Rainfall in. (mm)

Pretoria: average rainfall

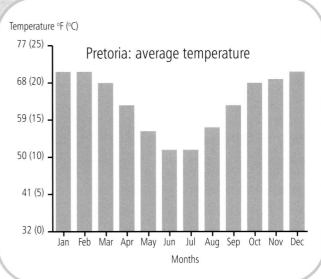

Temperature °F (°C)

Pretoria: average temperature

Population and health

In 2008, South Africa had a population of around 48.8 million people. This is double what it was in 1970. However, population growth has now slowed. In some places, it has reversed because of the high number of deaths caused by a disease called HIV and AIDS.

Rainbow nation

South Africa is sometimes called the rainbow nation. This is because there is a wide mix of people living there. People have been moving to South Africa for hundreds of years. Many European settlers moved to South Africa. The Dutch, for example, founded Cape Town in the 1600s. In the 1800s, it became an English colony. Dutch and English colonists brought workers to South Africa, often from other colonies they controlled. People from India and Southeast Asia came to work in South Africa and never left. Today, these communities are part of modern South Africa. The blending of different cultures can be seen in the people, building styles, and foods of the country.

Facts at a glance

Total population: 48.8 million

Life expectancy at birth: 48.9

Children dying before the age of five: 6.9%

Ethnic composition:
black African 79%
white 9.6%
mixed race 8.9%
Indian/Asian 2.5%

▼ South Africa has a young population. This means it will keep growing for many years as young people marry and begin their own families.

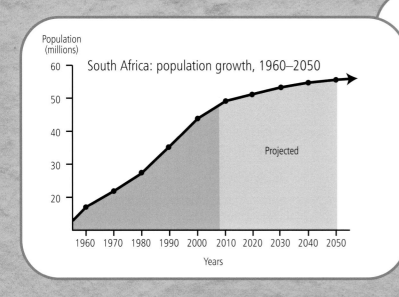

Population (millions)

South Africa: population growth, 1960–2050

60
50
40
30
20

Projected

1960 1970 1980 1990 2000 2010 2020 2030 2040 2050

Years

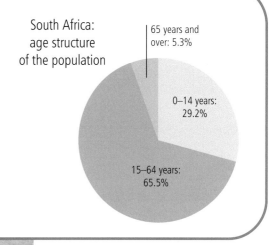

South Africa: age structure of the population

65 years and over: 5.3%

0–14 years: 29.2%

15–64 years: 65.5%

Kept apart

For many years the policy of apartheid, meaning "kept apart," split up different cultures into black, white, mixed race, and Asian. Housing, jobs, schools, hospitals, transportation, and even toilets were divided up. The best were given to the ruling white population. Although apartheid ended more than decade ago, South Africa is still trying to undo the harm it caused.

HIV and AIDS

HIV is a virus carried by humans that has no cure. HIV itself does not kill, but it can lead to AIDS, a disease that is deadly. HIV and AIDS is a major health problem in South Africa. In 2007, more than 350,000 people died from AIDS in South Africa. The government is trying to make sure people know about the virus. It is also trying to provide medicines that help to stop HIV from developing into AIDS.

DID YOU KNOW? People in South Africa don't live as long as they once did. In 1992, the average life span was 63, almost 15 years longer than it is now. HIV and AIDS is to blame for the change.

▶ A nurse (left) talks to an AIDS patient about the kinds of medicine she can take to help her with the disease.

Settlements and living

During apartheid, the South African government decided where people could live. Most of the black and mixed race (called "colored" in South Africa) population were sent to live in separate areas called townships. Since apartheid was stopped in 1994, people have had greater freedom to choose where they live. The government is working to fix the unequal treatment of the past. It hopes to make life better for everyone.

Urbanization

Following the end of apartheid, many people chose to move to cities. They went there to find jobs or join family already living there. About 60 percent of South Africans now live in cities. More people are moving to cities each year. The government built 2.4 million new homes from 2005–7 to try and keep up with the need for places to live. Despite this, many people who move to the cities end up living in poor-quality houses. This is especially true for those who were treated badly during apartheid.

⬤ Johannesburg is the largest city in South Africa and a major business center.

Facts at a glance

Urban population: 60% (29.3 million)

Rural population: 40% (19.5 million)

Population of largest city: 3.4 million (Johannesburg)

City life

Johannesburg and Cape Town are the largest cities in South Africa. Each has more than 3 million people. Every day, new people move to these cities to find jobs. Many build homes from whatever they can find. They put up these homes in large, crowded areas outside the city. These areas are sometimes called slums, or shantytowns. They often have no public services such as electricity, water, drains, and garbage collection. They are also often a long way from schools, doctors, jobs, and stores.

During apartheid, social separation was based on skin color. Now it is based on money. Rich people of all ethnicities separate themselves from the poor. This has led to high rates of crime in some areas. Some people live in gated communities with fences and armed guards to protect them.

⬤ A woman collects water from a standpipe. Many people in South Africa do not have their own water supply in their homes.

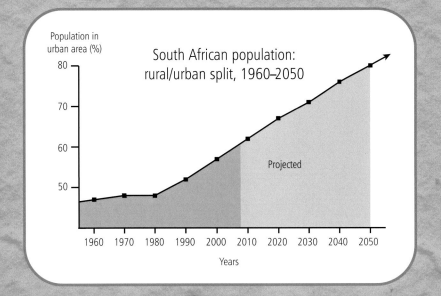

Population in urban area (%)

South African population: rural/urban split, 1960–2050

80

70

60

50

Projected

1960 1970 1980 1990 2000 2010 2020 2030 2040 2050

Years

DID YOU KNOW?
South Africa has some of the highest crime levels in the world. In 2006–7, there were 19,202 reported murders, 200,000 robberies, and more than 430,000 assaults.

Family life

The family has always been an important part of life in South Africa. However, apartheid and HIV and AIDS have hurt families.

Living apart

Apartheid forced many families to live apart. Men were forced to work in mines or factories, away from their families. Today many families are still separated. A family member often has to move to a faraway city, mine, or commercial farm to find work. Most separated families come from the countryside. It is common to find homes there with only one adult, usually the mother, caring for the children.

Family size

In the past, family members from more than one generation would live together or near one another. But with family members moving away for work or to cities, this pattern of living is less common now. Although families are becoming smaller and more spread out, there are still many homes where grandparents live with a family and help care for children while parents are working.

▼ The average family size in South Africa has been falling as population growth slows. Most urban families now have just two or three children.

South Africans get married, on average, when they are 29. This is similar to the average age of marriage in Europe and the United States. But it is higher than in other African countries. It is not unusual for women to have children before they marry.

Missing family

HIV and AIDS has had a big effect on families in South Africa. Most people with HIV and AIDS are adults. Many are parents. This has led to a situation where more grandparents look after children whose parents have died. It has also led to millions of children becoming orphans because there is no one left to care for them.

▶ This ten-year-old boy lives with his grandmother because his mother died from AIDS.

DID YOU KNOW?

In an average South African classroom of 30 children, two students will have lost at least one parent to AIDS.

Religion and beliefs

When Europeans first arrived in South Africa in around 1650, they brought their Christian beliefs with them. Missionaries later followed to spread Christianity among local people. Today, Christianity is the country's main religion, and around 80 percent of South Africans are Christians. Churches are an important part of community life in South Africa. Many churches offer lively services that combine religious teachings with dancing, singing, and healing.

Other religions

Hinduism and Islam both arrived in South Africa through trade and workers who were brought to South Africa during its time as a colony. One of the country's oldest and best-known Muslim communities is Bo-Kaap, an area of Cape Town. This is where people who came from Indonesia settled and built South Africa's first mosque. They are today known as the Cape Malay community. The community is famous for its bright buildings and friendly people, and these have made the area popular with visitors to Cape Town.

A worshiper sings inside her church in Leseding Township. Singing and dancing plays an important role in many of South Africa's local churches.

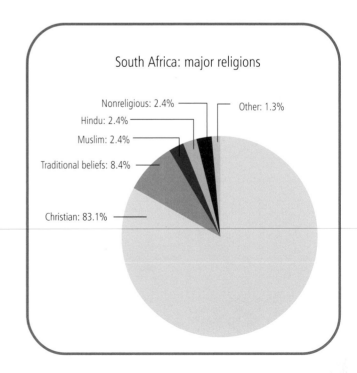

South Africa: major religions

Nonreligious: 2.4%
Hindu: 2.4%
Muslim: 2.4%
Traditional beliefs: 8.4%
Other: 1.3%
Christian: 83.1%

Beliefs and festivals

Various festivals take place in South Africa. Some celebrate successful harvests and give thanks to the land. These include the Riebeek Kasteel Olive Festival in the Western Cape and the Prickly Pear Festival in Nelson Mandela Bay. Healing rituals remain an important feature in the religious life of many South Africans.

National holidays

When apartheid ended and South Africa began rebuilding, five new national holidays were created, and one had its name changed. The new holidays all mark important moments or events in the struggle for equality. They include Human Rights Day, Freedom Day, Youth Day, National Women's Day, Heritage Day, and the Day of Reconciliation.

▼ Bo-Kaap is one of South Africa's oldest settlements and the first area in which Muslims settled. It has ten mosques including the first in South Africa which was built in 1798.

DID YOU KNOW?

Each year the Cape Malay community holds the Cape Town Minstrel Carnival that dates back to 1848. Groups of people paint their faces white, play music, and sing songs.

CHURCH
CHIAPPINI

Education and learning

Like everything else in South Africa, most schools were segregated during apartheid. Only white people were allowed to go to the best schools. In South Africa today, schools are seen as a way to create a more equal country.

Learning for the future

During apartheid, almost one quarter of South Africans did not go to school. Most of those who did not attend school were black. Now everyone can go to school. In poor areas, schools are often bad, and in cities, they are often crowded. Despite these problems, most children go to primary school and secondary school.

▼ Children play water polo during sports class in a mixed-race private school in Johannesburg.

In South Africa, school is free, and it is compulsory for children up to 16 years old (grade 9) to go to school. But the cost of traveling or books and uniforms can make it too expensive for some children. They are unable to go to school. Other children are kept out of school so they can work.

Universities

Most of South Africa's university system was segregated, too. However, now students can go to any university they choose. New universities have been created since 1994 to keep up with the numbers of new students. There are more black and mixed-race teachers as well. Today, most large South African cities have at least one university.

Skills-based learning

Colleges across South Africa offer a variety of classes. Students can learn skills such as building, computing, and farming. Some colleges teach adults who could not attend school during apartheid. The classes help students to find jobs. They are often run in local communities or by small charities or the government.

⬤ This woman is learning how to bake as part of a training program for unemployed women.

DID YOU KNOW?
Many children have to care for sick relatives who have AIDS. A new subject in South African schools called Life Skills teaches pupils how to look after themselves and others around them.

Employment and economy

South Africa is Africa's strongest economy. It is the only African country that is in the world's top 30 economies. Nevertheless, many people in South Africa do not have jobs. Millions of others work in jobs with low pay.

A diverse economy

Most African countries make money through farming or mining. This means that if the world price for minerals falls or there is poor weather, their economies can suffer greatly. But South Africa has more kinds of products than other countries.

It is a leading exporter of high-value crops such as spices, flowers, and wine. It is also one of the biggest producers of gold and diamonds.

In addition, South Africa has many factories and a fast-growing service sector. This includes banking, insurance, and telecommunications, as well as health, education, and local services.

Tourism is another part of the service sector. Twice as many people visit South Africa now than they did during the time of apartheid. In 2007, more than 8.5 million tourists visited South Africa.

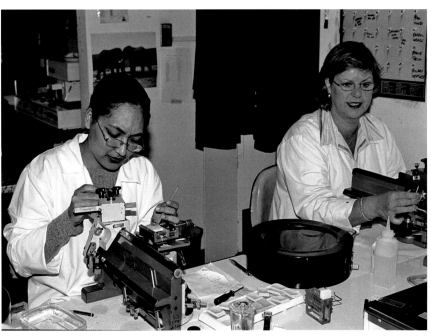

⚠ These people work in a medical laboratory. South Africa has more professional jobs like this than other African countries.

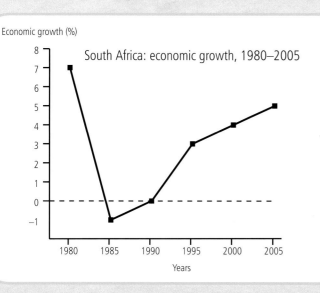

Economic growth (%)

South Africa: economic growth, 1980–2005

Years

Global center

Many companies that want to operate in Africa choose South Africa as a base. The country has reliable roads, a good communications system, and educated workers. Cape Town and Johannesburg in particular have many international insurance and communications companies and banks.

Employment problems

Almost a quarter of South African workers are out of work, but in some areas, this can be as high as half. Being out of work is a common problem among young men from poor and black communities. Being out of work has been linked to growing rates of crime.

A lack of jobs is a problem in other ways, too. Many people work in jobs that do not make the most of their skills. The government is trying to tackle such problems by attracting businesses to set up in South Africa. It also helps individuals and groups to create their own business by offering funding or training.

⬤ People who sell goods from the side of the road in Cape Town are among those not included in official employment figures.

Industry and trade

Factories employ around a quarter of South Africa's work force. A wide range of goods made in South Africa is traded around the world. Nearly one-third of the country's income comes from these goods.

South Africa's treasures

Mining is important in South Africa. The country is famous for its gold and diamonds. Such treasures first lured Europeans to South Africa in the 1800s. Gold and diamonds are still mined, but today, South Africa is the biggest producer of metals such as platinum and chromium. Iron ore, copper, silver, and titanium are other important metals for South Africa. The country meets many of its own energy needs through its vast coal supplies. It has so much coal that it exports some of it to Europe and East Asia as well.

▼ A miner works deep underground in a gold mine near Johannesburg.

Trade links

South Africa's rich land and position on major shipping routes make it a key trade partner for many other countries. Most of its exports are metals or foods, and its imported goods include machines, chemicals, equipment, and oil. As well as handling the country's own trade, South African ports import and export goods for neighboring African countries. Ships also use South African ports as a stopping point to collect or drop off goods before returning or continuing their journeys.

 A large cargo ship waits in Durban, one of South Africa's most important ports.

Factories

Most factories in South Africa use natural resources to make products for export. For example, steel is used to build ships and make vehicles. Textiles, electronic goods, and chemicals are some of the other products made in South Africa. Food processing is also important to the economy. South Africa is also a major producer of weapons. Its factories use expertise in explosives first developed in the mining industry.

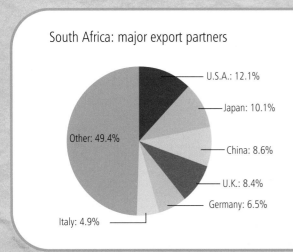

South Africa: major export partners

- U.S.A.: 12.1%
- Japan: 10.1%
- China: 8.6%
- U.K.: 8.4%
- Germany: 6.5%
- Italy: 4.9%
- Other: 49.4%

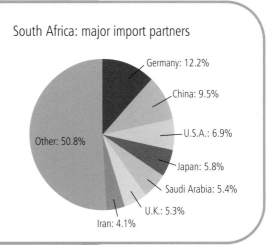

South Africa: major import partners

- Germany: 12.2%
- China: 9.5%
- U.S.A.: 6.9%
- Japan: 5.8%
- Saudi Arabia: 5.4%
- U.K.: 5.3%
- Iran: 4.1%
- Other: 50.8%

Farming and food

Almost 85 percent of South Africa's land is not used for growing crops because of poor soil and a lack of water. This means that on the land that is used, there is great competition between growing food for local needs and growing crops for export.

Cash crops

Large-scale farming in South Africa focuses on producing food for export or for processing. These are known as cash crops. Fruits such as apples, oranges, mangoes, and melons are popular export crops, as are vegetables such as okra, chilies, peas, and beans. Corn, wheat, peanuts, sugar cane, and sorghum are the key crops for large farms. They are mostly exported or used for food processing. South African farms also grow flowers that

Facts at a glance

Farmland: 13% of total land area

Main agricultural exports: Wine, grapes, oranges

Main agricultural imports: Rice, wheat, soybeans

Average daily calorie intake: 2,940 calories

A woman checks vines in a vineyard of the Cape region. This is where most of South Africa's wine is produced.

are exported to Europe and the United States. Grapes grown in South Africa are used for wine. South Africa was the world's seventh-largest wine producer in 2005.

Family farming

Smaller-scale farming, where farmers produce food for their own needs or for sale in local markets, is still popular in the countryside. Corn and millet are the main crops, together with vegetables such as cabbages, tomatoes, potatoes, and beans. Some families also keep animals for food, such as goats, sheep, cattle, and chickens.

Meat and fish

Meat and fish are a key part of the South African diet. Beef cattle and some sheep are the main animals used for food. Fishing is important off the southern and western coasts. Large fish stocks can be found there.

Diet and food

The average calorie intake of South Africans is similar to that in many parts of Europe. This hides the fact that many South Africans suffer from hunger, especially in poorer communities. The diet has many different cultural influences. Local foods include *bobotie*, a spicy ground meat dish served with yellow rice, and *biltong*, cured meat. The *braai*, or barbecue, is also popular with South Africans for cooking a wide variety of meat, fish, and vegetables.

⬤ Tuna is offloaded at Cape Town docks. Fish is an important part of the South African diet.

Transportation and communications

Transportation in South Africa is better than in the rest of Africa, but mainly connects the larger towns and cities. Beyond this, it becomes less reliable. Cell phones have made communication much easier in South Africa. More people are using the Internet, too.

Long-distance travel

The paved roads that connect South Africa's major cities provide key routes for trade and business. However, around 80 percent of roads are unpaved. In poor weather, it is not possible to use some roads. South Africa has the world's fourteenth-largest railroad network. It is bigger than that of the U.K. or Spain. Like its roads, South Africa's

Facts at a glance

Total roads: 224,998 miles (362,099 km)
Paved roads: 45,675 miles (73,506 km)
Railroads: 12,969 miles (20,872 km)
Major airports: 15
Major ports: 5

⬇ Major roads provide fast transportation links between major cities. This new interchange and highway is in Gauteng province.

Local travel

In much of South Africa, people travel by foot, bicycle, or shared vehicles such as minibuses and large cars. In towns and cities, there are also regular bus services. Local train services run in five city centers, including Johannesburg, Cape Town, and Durban. Around 1.7 million passengers use the services every weekday. Some people refuse to use them because of fears about crime.

Across much of South Africa travelers use shared taxis. These are often minibuses and normally travel on set routes that are off the main bus network. They leave when they are full instead of having a regular timetable.

Communication revolution

Cell phone and Internet use have grown rapidly in South Africa, though Internet use is limited mainly to cities and wealthier people. The increase in communications has created many new business opportunities. South African companies are now Africa's leading supplier of communications goods such as cell phones.

🔺 Cell phones are common today in South Africa.

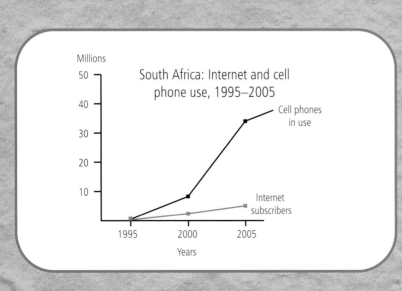

Millions

South Africa: Internet and cell phone use, 1995–2005

Cell phones in use

Internet subscribers

1995   2000   2005

Years

DID YOU KNOW?
South Africa's main cell phone company is called MTN. It operates in 20 countries across Africa and the Middle East. It expects to have 300 million customers by 2012!

Leisure and tourism

South Africa's beautiful land, national parks, and fine beaches make it a very popular tourist destination. Local people also enjoy outdoor activities such as hiking and surfing. Other popular leisure activities include sports, music, and going to the movies.

Music and film

Music has long been a part of South African culture. Jazz is especially popular and has developed its own particular style. Some of South Africa's biggest music stars have become internationally famous, such as Ladysmith Black Mambazo, Miriam Makeba, and Hugh Masekela. Local forms of music include *kwaito,* a lively type of hip-hop music that began in black areas. Movie theaters are popular in South Africa and the country has its own small filmmaking industry. Local movies explore the hardships of apartheid or township life. The South African film *Tsotsi* won an Oscar for Best Foreign Language Film in 2006.

A sports-loving nation

South Africa is a sports-loving nation. During apartheid, sports were segregated. Cricket and rugby were almost entirely played by white people. Soccer, boxing, and track events were played mainly by black people. White people had more access to sports.

Facts at a glance
Tourist arrivals (millions)

1995	4.5
2000	5.9
2005	7.4
2006	8.4

These musicians are playing traditional music. Jazz and pop are also popular musical styles in South Africa.

26

There was less support for black people to play sports. Sports are now used to help bring communities together. Sports facilities are gradually being improved across the country.

International sports

South Africa has many world-class athletes. During the time of apartheid, the country was banned from many international competitions. In 1995, South Africa was welcomed back to international sports when it hosted the Rugby World Cup. Its team, the Springboks, went on to win. They won the same competition again in 2007. In 1996, South Africa's national soccer team won the Africa Cup of Nations. In 1998, it qualified for the World Cup Finals for the first time.

Tourism

South Africa is the leading tourist destination in Africa. Most tourists stay in just a few areas including Cape Town, the Kruger National Park, and KwaZulu. This means only some areas benefit from tourism. A new type of "township tourism" means that people can visit townships to find out about the life of many ordinary South Africans.

An elephant walks along the road in the Kruger National Park, South Africa's most famous national park.

DID YOU KNOW?

In 2010, South Africa will become the first African country to host the soccer World Cup. This sports event is the world's biggest, apart from the Olympics!

Environment and wildlife

South Africa's environment varies from mountains to deserts and from coasts to grasslands. Its wildlife is just as diverse. South Africa faces a major challenge in protecting its environment from human activities.

Wildlife

African wildlife, such as elephants, lions, cheetahs, buffalo, giraffes, and zebras, can be found in South Africa. Today, wildlife is mainly limited to national parks such as the Kruger National Park in the northeast of the country. There are also some private game parks and reserves.

The beaches around Cape Town where penguins live are another popular wildlife attraction. In 1983, there were only a few breeding penguins left, but a successful program to save them has increased their numbers to more than 3,600.

DID YOU KNOW?
The oceans around South Africa are among the best places in the world to see great white sharks. These powerful creatures were made famous by the Hollywood movie *Jaws*.

Facts at a glance

Proportion of area protected: 5.3%
Biodiversity (known species): 24,569
Threatened species: 140

▼ African penguins are a popular attraction on Boulders Beach near Cape Town.

A floral kingdom

The region around Cape Town is home to the Cape Floral Kingdom. Also called "fynbos," it is a rare habitat found only in this area. It has more than 7,700 kinds of plants. This means that in terms of its size, the Cape Floral Kingdom has more kinds of plants than the Amazon rain forest. Around 70 percent of its plants are found nowhere else in the world. One of the most famous flowers from this kingdom is the King Protea. This is the national flower of South Africa and has flowers up to 12 inches (30 centimeters) across.

⬭ The King Protea is the national flower of South Africa and one of the most famous species in the Cape Floral Kingdom.

Protecting the environment

Growing human populations, together with mining and factories, have all had an impact on South Africa's environments. One major problem is the increasing amount of waste that has been dumped on land and rivers across the country. Some local communities have responded to this by finding ways to recycle waste into new and useful products. The government is also helping. In 2003, it introduced a ban on thin plastic bags because of the damage they were causing to the environment.

⬭ This man is collecting and sorting waste at a center for recycling. Recycling is one way that South Africa is trying to protect the environment.

29

Glossary

administrative relating to the management of something

apartheid system of keeping people of different races apart

calorie intake way of measuring how much people eat. A calorie is a unit of food energy.

climate normal weather conditions of an area

colony country controlled by another country

colored term used in South Africa to describe people of mixed race

commercial related to business

communications use of telephones, the Internet, or media to communicate with others

compulsory something that must be done

culture way of life and traditions of a group of people

cured way of preserving meat, often by drying or salting it

export goods or service that is sold to another country

food processing making of raw food into another food product, such as apples into apple juice

game park area where wild animals are protected or bred

gated communities groups that live behind protective fences and walls

GDP total value of goods and services produced by a country

habitat place where a plant or animal usually lives

healing process of becoming well or curing somebody

HIV and AIDS Human Immunodeficiency Virus (HIV) is a virus that has no cure. It can develop into Acquired Immune Deficiency Syndrome (AIDS), which will kill people.

import goods or service that is bought from another country

insurance protection against risk

judicial system of law in a country

landscapes physical features (such as mountains, rivers, deserts) of a place

legislative branch of government that creates the laws of a country

mineral solid substance that is found in rocks or the ground. Salt, gold, and limestone are examples of minerals.

missionaries people who travel to other countries to preach Christian beliefs

mosque Muslim place of worship

natural resources water, soil, trees, and minerals that are found naturally in an area

Oscar annual award given by the U.S. film industry

parliament group of people elected to make and enforce the laws of a country

paved roads roads that have a hard stone or clay surface

plateau large, flat area of raised land

prickly pear tropical cactus that produces pear-shaped fruit

segregated kept apart

service sector part of the economy that provides services such as banking, retail, education, and healthcare

sorghum food plant that produces a grain that is widely eaten in Africa

township area in South Africa where black people were settled during apartheid

virus small organism that is the cause of a disease or illness

Topic web

Use this topic web to explore South African themes in different areas of study.

History
Find out what you can about apartheid. List the things that made apartheid unfair for black people.

Geography
Find out how many countries there are in Africa. Look at their size and population. Where does South Africa rank in relation to other African countries?

Science
South Africa has many important minerals, including coal. Find out how coal is formed and how it is mined. Why is coal a nonrenewable resource?

Math
Find out how many South African rand there are in $1. Choose some items (e.g. a bottle of water, an apple) and work out how much they would cost you in rand.

South Africa

English
Think of three questions about living in South Africa you have after reading this book. Write a letter to a child in South Africa to find out the answers to these questions.

Citizenship
Many people in South Africa are poor. What do we mean when we use the word "poverty?" Create a spider diagram to explore what you understand by poverty.

Design and Technology
Many people in South Africa use waste products to create new and useful products—even toys. Collect some waste products from your home or school. What could you design and make with them?

Information Technology
Use the Internet to find out when is the best time to go on vacation to South Africa and what are the main things to see.

Further Information, Web Sites, and Index

Further reading

Letters From Around the World: South Africa by Cath Senker (Cherrytree Books, 2005)
South Africa: The Culture by Domini Clark (Crabtree Publishing Company, 2008)
Welcome to South Africa by Umaima Mulla-Feroze (Gareth Stevens Publishing, 2002)

Web Sites

Due to the changing nature of Internet links, PowerKids Press has developed an online list of Web sites related to the subject of this book. This site is updated regularly. Please use this link to access this list:
http://www.powerkidslinks.com/discovc/southa/

Index